The A - Z Guide To The Latest
AGE-REJUVENATION
Products & Procedures

AN ACTION E-BOOK PUBLICATION

Action E-Books provide the very latest discoveries and information in a concise format, their purpose being that you may start fulfilling your desires now via the reading experience. Our motto is: Time & tide waits for no one, so do it now, for waiting is a total waste of time and energy.

ISBN-13: 978-1523260614
ISBN-10: 1523260610

DEDICATED TO DURGA

CONTENTS

Introduction – Secrets To A Younger You

THE A – Z INDEX:

Ancient Wisdoms Of The Mystical Traditions

Introduction – Secrets To A Younger You

We stand at the threshold of the greatest revolution in the science of age rejuvenation.

Subsequently, the relative products and procedures available in today's market are many and varied. The Action E-book, *The Complete Guide To The Latest AGE-REJUVENATION Products & Procedures,* catalogues these, inclusive of the relevant information, in order to assist in your choice as to which ones may best suit your needs. This book, *The A -Z Guide To The Latest AGE-REJUVENATION Products & Procedures,* is a fast abbreviated guide – more or less a dictionary, so to speak – for conveniently efficient reference purposes.

All of these products have one thing in common; they seek to treat our cellular networks – to stimulate and revitalize them. At the end of the day, they are all focused on the same objective; the rejuvenation of our cells, so that we can look, feel and be younger.

In the past decade, remarkable technological advancements and scientific discoveries have provided us with unprecedented insight into the aging process. This is leading us to staggering breakthroughs within the field of anti-aging. The biggest breakthrough in the field came in 2003 when the *Human Genome Project* was completed. It provided the platform in allowing us to view the aging process in a revolutionary way, and offered us the ability to see how the body ages at a genetic level.

The known causes of aging are: cell loss – cell stagnation – cell waste accumulation – cell power loss – cell mutation – cell protein cross-link. Simply put, aging happens when miscommunication occurs within the cells, and they lose their ability to function effectively over time, due to a loss of energy and efficiency within them, causing our telomeres – telomeres considered to be the key to aging – to shorten. This is mainly brought about by a buildup of waste products at a greater rate than our cells can eliminate them, causing cell weakening over time that is the cause of age related illnesses and aging as we know it.

If our cells could maintain their ability to eliminate waste products faster than the build-up of this waste, while maintaining their energy and efficiency without losing their power, and thus retain their ability to communicate with each other effectively, we would then preserve our youthfulness and elude the aging process.

Telomeres are considered the key to slowing down, or stopping, the aging process.

Telomeres are the protective caps on the ends of chromosomes, which determine how the cells in our bodies age. They are a mixture of our DNA and our proteins that protect the ends of our chromosomes, helping them to remain stable. As they shorten they weaken, which causes the cells to age and then die. They shorten as our cells age, but scientific research has found that telomeres can, in fact, lengthen, improving our health and longevity – effectively reversing the aging process.

Research results, claimed to be of a major significant breakthrough, show that just one way to lengthen telomeres is in particular lifestyles. Meditation, diet, exercise, stress management and social interaction are ingredients shown to improve the length of our telomeres. So we can intervene to lengthen our telomeres over time. Therefore, our genes and telomeres as they are presently, may not necessarily be our fate as it is possible to increase the lengths of our telomeres by our lifestyle choices, reclaiming our health and living a longer more youthful life.

The research indicates that if we follow a lifestyle based on the principles of:

- a diet high in whole foods, plant based proteins, fruits & vegetables, unrefined grains, low in fat (10% of calories) and low in refined carbohydrates,

- moderate aerobic exercise, such as walking 30 minutes a day 6 days a week,

- gentle yoga-based stretching, breathing or meditation for 60 minutes daily,

- and increased social networking, such as weekly support group sessions that include moderate exercise, stress management training & counselling,

then in 3 months we should expect to significantly increase our telomerase activity – telomerase being an enzyme which repairs and lengthens telomeres – thus reversing our aging process.

Today, amazingly, there is some forty billion dollars presently directed at research into anti-aging. We are told, we will probably soon all have the ability to print 3D skin cells in order to refresh our appearances, and the ability to print new 3D body parts to replace our sick ones. Reliable predictions are being made already that those in their 20's and 30's today can expect to live to a very healthy and active 150 years of age – and still look good.

Perfect wrinkle free skin. Surely this is not a lot to ask for, considering skin is our largest single organ that contains the rest of our anatomy within it. Flawless skin – obtaining it is soon going to become considerably easier.

Through the vast sums of capital being made available by powerful investors – such as, for example: Google whose subsidiary Google Calico is solely devoted to the aging process, Oracle billionaire Larry Ellison's Ellison Medical Foundation that supports research exploring the biology of aging, billionaire Peter Nygård and stem cell research, billionaire Tan Sri Lim Kok Thay financial backer of Human Longevity dedicated to longevity through genomics and cell therapy technology, and many more – great innovative anti-aging science is evolving rapidly. This goes well beyond the desire for us to look younger, which most certainly is a major requirement. It also extends to realistically energizing ourselves with youthfulness and actually feeling and being youthful. It is appearing that due to an understanding at the genetic level, and the products and procedures subsequently developed, the desired results of the age-old quest for immortality are now upon us.

So what are the secrets to younger looking skin? It appears the answer to this question lies in making the skin as tough as we possibly can – so that it can take whatever our lifestyle throws at it and simply bounce back.

We expose our skin to all sorts of stresses like pollution, sun, wind, smoke washing, rubbing, scrubbing, and applying numerous cocktails of chemicals, lotions and make-up etc. that affect our skin's appearance and function. If it is damaged it appears dull, dry, and lifeless, resulting in being sensitive to light and sun damage that prematurely ages it. In order to have youthful skin we need to first build strong skin, and this means we need to find balance between focusing our attention on the strengthening of our skin and its layers, while controlling the damage we are doing to it.

The bottom line here is, we have to safeguard our skin's barrier, and it appears using powerful antioxidants is the best bet. These antioxidants go in search of the damaging free radicals created during the negative exposure of our skin to the elements. When these free radicals get into our skin they attack the collagen and elastin that keep the skin smooth and supple.

So what do we look for to ensure we have the best available cover? Firstly, it appears a product that contains a mix of antioxidants, including fat soluble ones like vitamin A and E, and water soluble ones like vitamin C, as all of these vitamins nourish different parts within our skin's cells.

The serums available are designed for all skin types and are absorbed quickly into the skin delivering the highest concentrations of the active ingredients – named on the packaging.

Vitamin A is the number one pick when it comes to addressing every aging issue of the skin. It is available within over-the-counter Retinol products and prescription products like Retin A. Vitamin A travels through to the 2nd layer of the skin, the dermis, where it activates fibroblasts that create collagen and then builds up the structure within the skin.

It is recommended that antioxidant products are applied twice daily – in the morning and at night – after the skin has been cleaned, and that the morning application should be followed with a sunscreen. Also recommended; antioxidants may be used immediately after sun exposure as scientific research shows this helps the skin considerably because sun damage continues for some hours after the exposure.

Protecting our skin from the unavoidable exposures of daily living from the outside unfortunately falls short. We need to also nourish the skin from the inside out in order for it to grow stronger – for us to really be biologically younger, rather than just look younger. It is really important for us to repair our skin and stimulate new stronger growth. That is where peptides and growth factors come into the equation as they help stimulate collagen production, which in turn shows remarkable results.

Even more significant is the in-depth research into DNA repairing enzymes. Around the age of 35 our enzyme levels begin to decline, weakening our skin and making it more susceptible to damage from the elements. Research has shown that products with DNA repair enzymes actually reverse the damage done to our skin, and in turn help to rebuild it by way of thickening it as these products limit the growth of collagenase – an enzyme which damages collagen production and degrades it over time.

Then there is the fatty tissue, between the skin's cells, which acts like a glue by holding the skin together. When this glue, or fatty tissue, begins to weaken we experience aging of the skin as over time it becomes inflexible, so we need to stimulate the skin by replenishing the fatty tissue between the cells. To do this we need a range of lipids. These can be obtained via our diet from foods such as salmon and fatty fish, helped with foods that contain high levels of moisturizing ingredients such as butter, fatty acid oils and hyaluronic acid.

The following, *A – Z Guide To The Latest Age-Rejuvenation Products & Procedures,* catalogues basically what is available to assist in the processes relating to age-rejuvenation – the partner book, *The Complete Guide To The Latest Age-Rejuvenation Products & Procedures*, provides more in-depth information – as always, it is advisable to read the list of ingredients on the product packaging, where applicable, in order to identify the correct choices as to our personal requirements. When considering professional treatments, the recommended advice is, also as always, to ask questions and feel free to obtain a second opinion. Now, as the future of perfect skin may have arrived, let's look at the specific ways in which we can build it, along with beautiful, healthy, youthful minds and bodies.

THE A-Z INDEX

Acupuncture Facelift

The Acupuncture Facelift is relatively new in our modern beauty industry, but there are records of Acupuncture Facial Rejuvenation being used in the service of beauty for centuries. It is a form of painless, ancient Chinese medicine that originated more than 2,000 years ago, in which fine needles are inserted into the skin at certain points on the face and body. The needles are inserted at vortex points where energy is travelling to and from organs along lines called meridians, which causes your energy to flow more efficiently. When energy flows more efficiently, circulation is improved, and endorphins are released, helping the body rejuvenate.

The ability of acupuncture to improve a variety of skin conditions has now been documented in clinical studies. This treatment entails no incisions, and practitioners claim it can reduce wrinkles, eliminate fine lines, lift sagging skin and improve skin color and texture. Patients have reported the reduction or erasure of fine lines, and the softening of deeper ones over time, the firming of jowls, a reduction in the size of under-eye bags, enhanced skin tone, increased energy and eyes that sparkle.

Alpha Hydroxy Acids (AHA)

AHA's exfoliate by way of dissolving the glue that holds surface skin cells together so dead cells are removed to reveal youthful skin – this process encourages cell turnover that otherwise slows with aging. They allow better absorption of moisturizers, serums and general skin treatments and assist with the treatment of brown spots and wrinkles.

Alpha-Lipoic Acid

The body makes this acid in every cell we have. As an antioxidant, it attacks free radicals throughout the body. It is a substance that is commercially touted as reducing wrinkles, reducing fine lines and evening out pores, giving skin a healthy glow.

Antioxidants & The Free Radical Theory of Aging

When applied to the skin, antioxidants prevent free radical damage. According to the free radical theory of aging, topical antioxidants are extremely powerful skin care ingredients that play a very important part in our anti-aging skin care regime. The Free Radical Theory of Aging; when oxygen is used to make energy in human cells, it releases reactive oxygen species (ROS), commonly known as free radicals, which are fought by our cells natural defenses called antioxidants. Many antioxidants can now be extracted or synthesized into tablets, creams or serums – anti-aging technology.

Antioxidants

Antioxidants are nutrients that when ingested, or applied to the skin by way of cream or serum formulas, prevent free radical damage. They act by stopping the damage being done by free radicals that attack our skin's supply of collagen. Free radicals are unstable molecules that develop through exposure to: environmental damage such as pollution, and sun damage to the skin.

It is now well proven how powerful topical antioxidants can be in anti-aging, and consequently they are becoming a very significant cosmeceutical ingredient of the future. It is advised that they should be included in everybody's daily routine for healthier, youthful skin. Coffee berry is now believed to be the single most powerful source of antioxidant to date, and CoQ10, vitamin C and E stand out, significantly improving the appearance of lines and wrinkles. Retinoids, Niacinamide, Hyaluronic Acid, Alpha Hydroxy Acid, Salicylic Acid, L-ascorbic Acid, Alpha-Lipoic Acid, Avobenzone, and Alpha Hydroxy Acids (AHA) are also advantageous antioxidants used in some of the latest anti-aging technology skin care products.

Aquagold

Aquagold is a system used by some dermatologists which involves using 20 short thinner than a hair micro needles with channels that allow ingredients to seep into the skin's second layer, the dermis. This system can be used at any age to address dry tired skin. Sometimes referred to as a system that takes a prune and makes it look like a plum.

ATX-101: Injectable Fat Dissolver

ATX-101 – an injectable fat dissolving salt solution designed to tighten small stubborn pockets of fat such as double chins – shows very good results.

Avobenzone

This is a top-of-the-line skincare product, being a broad spectrum sunscreen with an SPF factor of 30 or higher. Avobenzone is a common chemical ingredient in sunscreen that blocks UVA rays. It is often paired with Benzophenone-3 or Oxybenzone to further strengthen the sheild against UVB rays. If you are adverse to chemicals, use a mineral block such as zinc oxide.

Bee Venom Extract

This natural anti-aging skin treatment is referred to as "Nature's Botox." It is claimed that it plumps and firms the skin, smooths wrinkles, and reduces scar tissue by way of stimulating the cells production of collagen and elastin. It contains a varied mix of naturally occurring proteins, peptides and amino acids, which have anti-inflammatory properties. The use of bee venom can be traced as far back as Ancient Greece, Egypt and China. One of the ingredients that makes this venom special lies within a peptide named melittin, which, it is claimed, increases the blood circulation on the areas of the skin applied, giving it a plumping effect, making wrinkles less visible. Also, it is used by some for treating and preventing acne due to its anti-bacterial properties. It caters for most skin types and is presently the in product amongst celebrities. It is produced by a sheet of glass being placed in close proximity to a beehive, and then an electrical current is discharged through it that entices the bees into stinging the glass, depositing some of their venom on it, which is scraped from the glass when there is a sufficient build-up of venom. It is noted that the bees are not harmed in any way throughout this process.

The cost of this product is $40-$80 a jar for products sourced from New Zealand – the leader in the bee venom extract process.

Belotero

Belotero is a new hyaluronic (filler) that is liquid-thin and colourless. Unlike traditional fillers, like Juvederm and Restylane that are quite thick, Belotero is so thin that it is ideally suited to the thinner skin around the breasts, and has so opened up a physician's ability to treat the cleavage area.

Botox

Botox is Botulinum Toxin type A – a neurotoxin that temporarily freezes a muscle's ability to contract. This injectable wrinkle eraser is considered among the most effective tools in the anti-aging arsenal. Presently Botox is the most popular and dramatic form of treatment in addressing frown lines, forehead lines, crows feet around the eyes and many other facial and neckline "imperfections." However, the quality of the end result will be determined by the skill of the applicator in injecting the Botox.

Botox – Depression

Could it be a shot at happiness? A study on depression associated with Georgetown University that involved using Botox injections found that 52% of patients felt significantly better. Could be something people seek out to erase wrinkles and feel a bit happier. For the nearly 14 million Americans who suffer from depression, "This could be the biggest thing since Prozac." It is claimed that Botox will become a standard treatment for depression in the future.

Botox – Gel

Reverance is a botulinum toxin gel dabbed onto your skin by doctor. It works just like the injectable version, and lasts for months.

Botox – Scalp Botox

Scalp Botox – to reduce and make certain sweat glands on the scalp inactive, so that your looks and comfort aren't ruined during a sweaty workout. It requires about 12-15 injections all over the scalp to prevent perspiration. It costs about $1000 and lasts for about 6mths.

Botox – Underarm sweating

Botox injections are being used as a temporary treatment for underarm sweating while creams are being developed for this purpose – as 20 or so injections in each armpit is not the most desirable experience.

Breast Lift – The Vampire Breast Lift

The Vampire Breast Lift (Dr Charles Runels) uses a combination of fillers and platelet-rich plasma to enhance the cleavage between the breasts, using one's own platelets and growth factors isolated from a small amount of one's own blood. This technique is used in the upper area of the breasts to plump, lift and round them so these areas look their best when visible in bras and bikinis etc. The procedure takes about 20-30 minutes.

Breasts: New Options – Belotero

For areas around our breasts that need treatment, there's now a new option – Belotero. This is a new hyaluronic (filler) that is liquid-thin and colourless, which has now opened up a physician's ability to treat the cleavage area. Unlike traditional fillers, like Juvederm and Restylane, which are quite thick, Belotero is so thin that it is ideally suited to the thinner skin around the breasts. The cost is $500 - $1,000 per syringe. Check with your professional provider as to the numbing agents available – as this filler does not in itself, as yet, have an inbuilt numbing agent.

Breasts: New Options – Stem Cell Breast Enlargement

An exciting revolution is taking place by way of a technique which uses stem cells to enlarge one's breasts, using one's own living tissue – not silicone.

The process relies on recent discoveries that human fat contains an amazing concentration of stem cells. These are separated by using a centrifuge system. Then tiny incisions are made in the skin for depositing the enriched fat cells, building the breast, injection at a time. A tool called a cell brush is used by the surgeon who repeatedly injects the enriched cells into the breast. Stem cells used can differentiate into new blood vessels, meaning the fat cells survive, and can be used as a natural way of reconstruction. So stem cells from new fat cells coax blood vessels to grow into new breast tissue. This was first done in 2004, when stem cells from fat were mixed with regular fat cells and then injected into the patient's breasts. The deposited tissue bonds quickly with the existing tissue. Within 48hrs the blood vessels and capillaries entwine with the new cells. Oxygen and nutrients are being supplied to the stable tissue. The injections aren't painful afterwards and patients go home the same day.

Further, scientists can now grow human fat cells in a laboratory for the first time – so patients could grow their own breast implants. Stem cells are turned into fat producing or adipose cells, which are put into plastic moulds to create different shapes and sizes of implants. Woman who are simply unhappy with their natural assets can now grow a new improved pair, with raw materials harvested from their own body fat, creating their desired cleavage.

Caffeine

Caffeine is also an antioxidant. Some people claim that it can have positive effects on skin, and certainly the evidence is quite promising when used on cellulite as it stimulates the cells' metabolism. Experts simply "don't know," but many companies have added it to lotions and creams, claiming it could be useful in the prevention of skin cancers, reducing wrinkles, and being an effective treatment for crows feet around the eyes.

Calorie Restriction

Calorie Restriction simply means eating less on a daily basis.

Calorie restriction has been referred to as being the real fountain of youth. Scientists who are usually cynical about anti-aging claims, actually agree that this method does indeed work, and that it greatly reduces the risk of many of our present day diseases – there is now an abundance of evidence that calorie restriction greatly reduces our chances of developing serious diseases, such as diabetes, cancer and heart diseases – as it allows our body cells to cleanse and revitalize themselves, leading to us living substantially longer and regaining youthfulness. It appears to be established that by eating less and exercising more, over the course of our lifetime, we can reduce, and even reverse, age-related cell and organ damage, consequently living a longer, healthier life.

Generally, the average healthy adult consumes approximately 2000 calories a day. There are many different approaches to calorie restriction. From straight out fasting for a number of days per week to a more moderate approach like a reduction of calories to 300 - 500 a day, which usually involves just cutting out those unnecessary extras.

Through the research done into calorie restriction, scientists are investigating and testing naturally occurring compounds that mimic the effects of calorie restriction – such as Resveratrol that is found in red wine, for example – as they think these compounds may restrict aging. It is considered that through this research we could expand our lifespans by up to 15 years within the next 40 years.

Cellulite

Cellulite is simply an enlarging of the fat cells that push upwards towards the soft tissues which lie just below the skin's surface, creating a dimpled uneven texture. Research shows that 85% of women over the age of 20 have it. Men too, suffer from cellulite, though only 10% are prone to it. It affects women on their bottoms and thighs of every shape and size, and there is no known cure for it. However, it can be treated using a variety of different procedures, some being a lot more effective than others.

Cellulite Treatments – Alternatives At Home

There is an abundance of affordable off-the-shelf treatments available, ranging from body brushes to foam rollers, creams and serums to using used coffee grounds as a body wash on the basis that caffeine and the antioxidants in coffee are known to be effective at decreasing the appearance of cellulite by way of increasing the area's circulation and reducing its water retention, and by releasing the stored-up toxins in the fat.

Some experts in the field recommend forsaking expensive treatments in favour of foods which strengthen the skin. Those foods for consideration are: generally brightly coloured fruits and vegetables for antioxidants that help prevent damage to the cells, whole wheat bread, brown rice and pasta that assist the digestive system in preventing the retention of water, tuna and salmon that provide the body with omega-3 fatty acids, which in turn clean the arteries and boost the body's circulation.

Cellulite Treatments – Bodysculpt

This treatment combines massage and meso-science, which is a state of the art virtual needle plus electroporation technology that is used to infuse potent and concentrated actives deeply into the skin. The therapist applies oil and cream onto the stubborn cellulite areas. A hand piece is used to massage the area to break down the cellulite through electrical waves which penetrate the cells. An oil is given – to apply morning and evening. The result to be expected is that the skin is a lot smoother after some 6 to 8 sessions.

Cellulite Treatments – Cellfina

Cellfina is a cellulite treatment that involves inserting a tiny needle-sized blade, 6-10mm, under the skin's surface to cut the fibrous bands that cause the rippling effect of cellulite, in order to smooth these bumps and lumps out. After the area to be treated has been numbed with an anaesthetic, a suction type cup is held on the area in order to stabilize it. Then the fibrous bands are snipped, releasing them. The treatment takes from 15 to 60 minutes, depending on the size of the area to be treated. The results have been described as nothing short of remarkable.

Cellulite Treatments – Hypoxi

This treatment combines advanced compression technology with exercise to get your body's natural system to burn the areas of fat and cellulite from the troubled areas. Each session starts with wearing a type of wetsuit costume, which sucks all the air out between it and you, and blows bubbles onto the hips, legs and stomach, increasing blood circulation in these areas. Then you are strapped into a machine, which looks like an exercise bike, and you cycle for 30 minutes while the machine continuously blows air in and sucks it out of your costume. This results in you staying at a regulated slow pace, which is optimum for your heart rate to function within its fat burning zone.

The results reported are that after some 3 weeks one can expect to see a difference in the texture and smoothness within the troubled areas. Weight loss is an added bonus.

Cellulite Treatments – I-Lipo

I-Lipo is a diode laser energy system, which stimulates the cells' energy batteries – the mitochondria. Electronic pads are placed on the areas to be treated, then a suction head is applied, which sucks the toxins to the skin's surface while increasing collagen to help smooth the cellulite. This system creates a chemical reaction which breaks down triglycerides into free fatty acids and glycerol. The intra-cellular fat is broken down and removed from the body through the lymphatic drainage system. The treatment includes a gel that is massaged into the bottom and thighs daily. Its active ingredient, actiporine, detoxifies the cells and stimulates the synthesis of collagen, while added caffeine shrinks fat cells and increases blood flow within the skin's structure. I-Lipo is painless and users have reported they are very pleased with the results.

Cellulite Treatments – Thermage

Thermage is radio frequency energy which heats the skin tissue at a deep level, reshaping it, while at the same time producing new collagen. The machine uses radio frequency waves against the skin, heating the deeper layers, stimulating the renewal of collagen. It is reported to have tightened skin tissues and structures almost immediately. Usually, the results – fat loss and smoother skin – are seen within a week. It is rated by some as the only treatment that has worked for them. It is also effective for the body generally, like the face, and eyes.

Chemical Peels

As an in-clinic treatment whereby a chemical solution is applied to the skin surface to exfoliate it and remove dead skin cells, chemical peel treatments vary in their intensity from mild to aggressive. The mild treatments are more hydrating and are used to infuse antioxidants and vitamin serums into the epidermis. The more aggressive treatments have to be highly controlled in order to protect the skin during the process. Patients can experience no peeling to flaking of the skin for up to 3-5 days and the skin is usually reddened by the treatment. The peels contain clinically proven retinols, L-lactic acid, AHA's and BHA's which exfoliate the skin, detoxify it and stimulate cellular renewal along with collagen production. This is an excellent form of treatment for sun damaged skin, aging skin and acne problems.

Chemical Peels – Alpha Hydroxy Acid Peels

This is a form of peel formulas using naturally occurring carboxylic acids.

Chemical Peels – Beta Hydroxy Acid Peels

These peels are being used more regularly as they aren't as strong as the Alpha Hydroxy Acids. This peel penetrates deeper into the skin which assists treatments for wrinkles and acne.

Chemical Peels – Croton Oil Peel

The active ingredient in this procedure is Croton Oil. It forms the basis of a deep peel process, which causes an intense, caustic, exfoliating reaction on the skin, resulting in regeneration of the dermal layer, restoring the dermis to a youthful state that no other peels can achieve. It requires sedation, either orally or intravenously.

Chemical Peels – Jessner's Peel

Developed by a dermatologist, it mixes Salicylic Acid 14%, Lactic Acid and Resorcinol in an Ethanol base. The beauty of this treatment is that it is very difficult to over treat the skin because of the mild doses used, its preparation, and because it does not penetrate as deeply as some other peels.

Chemical Peels – Retinoic Acid

This is a retinoid, and as such a deep peel, which is used in the removal of scars and wrinkles as well as skin pigmentation problems. This is a professional in-house treatment performed by a dermatologist or plastic surgeon. The patient leaves the treatment centre with the chemical solution on their face, and the peeling process occurs some 2-3 days later. Multiple peels can be performed over time in order to obtain dramatic results.

Chemical Peels – Used At Home

A chemical peel is a treatment wherein a chemical solution is applied in order to remove dead skin cells, which enables new skin to regenerate. The new skin is usually a lot smoother, and has less wrinkles than the old skin had. There are many different types of chemical peels, which can diminish many signs of aging on the face, hands, neck, and chest. Some types of mild chemical peels may be purchased over the counter to be used at home.

Collagen

Collagen is the most abundant protein within the human body. It is the most major component that connects tissue. It binds cells together and gives the skin its structure and its elasticity. As we age, collagen production within the body begins to decline, causing wrinkles, sagginess and a loss of the skin's elasticity generally.

Throughout history different cultures believe that eating collagen rich food will boost their skins' natural collagen levels. This is especially true throughout Asian countries, where the belief is prominent amongst women who have diets rich in collagen – and incidentally tend to have beautiful skin. In the U.S. eating skinless and boneless food has become a national obsession by many, so therefore their diets are virtually devoid of collagen.

Until recently there was no scientific proof which established any causal effect between collagen rich diets and beautiful skin. There is now growing proof that fully supports the theory that taking the right hydrolysed collagen peptides – which are essentially derived from poultry, fish, cows and pigs – will have extremely beneficial effects on our skin. The most convincing evidence of the benefits of collagen consumption was recently published in Skin Pharmacology and Physiology. Women who took 2.5 grams of a hydrolysed collagen peptide once a day for 8 weeks showed a 20% decrease in wrinkles around their eyes. Additionally the subject's levels of pro-collagen 1, the precursor to collagen, was up by some 60% - and these results were long lasting.

Copper – The Newly Acclaimed Super Skin Saver

Dermatologists agree, copper definitely plays an important part in maintaining healthy skin. It helps to develop collagen and elastin, which maintain the strength and firmness of the skin, and it promotes the production of hyaluronic acid, which assists sagging skin and wrinkles.

Also, it has antibacterial and antifungal properties, which help prevent infections.

Throughout history copper has been used as a prized metal. In Ancient Egypt the Ankh was the symbol for both eternal life and the sacred metal, copper. In India it has been treasured throughout history, not only for its beautifying qualities but also for its medicinal properties. It is claimed that drinking regularly from a copper vessel will induce certain powers and longevity.

Today it is beginning to become available in a variety of applications – from moisturizers and serums that contain new copper peptide formulas, to pillow cases embedded with microscopic copper particles that are absorbed by the skin while you sleep, to a dietary supplement that includes copper, which works with zinc and Vitamin C to form elastin. Copper peptides are being applied to eyebrow and eyelash enhancing systems, and to hair and anti-aging scalp serums to stimulate the collagen in hair follicles, which help promote thicker hair.

Dermal Fillers

Dermal fillers are principally made up from hyaluronic acid or collagen, and work by filling areas that require their volume to be restored. In other words, "plumping" these areas. This added volume gives the skin a younger, youthful looking appearance. With the advancements in the field of dermal fillers, they are now being described as "the liquid facelift."

The ones that are the safest to use fall under the category of non-permanent gels. They are made up of hyaluranon (a carbohydrate.) It is claimed, these are naturally occurring substances found in most living organisms, and as these substances decline as we age, these fillers are an ideal choice for rejuvenation.

These fillers are injected directly into the wrinkles and lines, principally on the face, but can be used in other body areas. When injected, the results are immediate because the treated area is filled to a degree where the wrinkle or effected area no longer exists.

The length of time these fillers last tends to vary from one individual to another. The thinner, softer fillers that are injected into the lips or fine lines will last for approximately 6 months. When the jawline, temple or cheeks are filled, the results can last a lot longer as a thicker, longer lasting version of the filler is used and should last for about a year – sometimes even 2 years or longer.

They are essentially very safe and effective when used correctly by experienced professionals and can correct wrinkles, lines, scars, and imperfections on the face. Due to the advancements being made in the science of dermal fillers they are now being used for shaping jaw lines, chins and lips as well as sculpting. Fillers have become a popular procedure in the anti-aging field and can certainly help in keeping the skin looking younger for longer.

Presently there is a new range of fillers being released on the market. These fillers are much thinner than previous fillers, and are much easier to smooth out, and less likely to give an over-filled appearance. Further, they can be used in sensitive areas, for instance around breast tissue. Belotero is a new hyaluronic filler, which is liquid thin and colourless. Another new filler to the market is Restylane Silk. It is formulated by using smaller and smoother particles. It is a much lighter form of dermal filler and does not over-plump the face. It works well for fine lines and offers a very natural appearance.

Dermal Rolling

Dermal Rolling is a non-surgical skin rejuvenation treatment. Dermal Rollers contain micro medical needles mounted on a roller, which create tiny punctures on the outer layers of the skin. These punctures stimulate specific growth factors of the skin, which in turn enhance collagen production within the cells, improve the skin's hydration system, blend scars on the skin's surface and assist in evening out pigmentation.

In clinical medical/cosmetic settings, Dermal Rolling is considered to be very effective for the reduction of wrinkles, fine lines and those annoying lines on the upper lip. It also tightens the skin, generally rejuvenates it, reduces scar tissue, improves the pores by reducing their size, and will further improve the skin's texture generally.

Dermal Rolling – Home Use Machines

Home care cosmetic Dermal Rollers, using smaller needles, are now available. These machines allow deeper absorption of skin nutrients contained in good quality skin creams and serums when applied afterwards. Usually the outer layers of the skin prevent the nutrients within products from penetrating the skin's dermis, or active layer, where the fibroblast cells reside that produce the all-important collagen. It is claimed that when applied after rolling, the penetration of product nutrients is increased from the normal 3% to 70%. This is due to the tiny micro channels which have been created between the layers of skin tissue.

Dermapen

The Dermapen is an electronically driven pen shaped device, being the very latest development in the Dermal Roller Evolution. It has been hailed as "the best recent innovation in skin rejuvenation," being a lot more precise than its predecessors, as it is equipped with fine vibrating needles that pierce the skin at a predetermined speed and depth, resulting in superior effects. The most revolutionary aspect of Dermapen is in its capability re dermal infusion – because when using Dermapen in conjunction with quality creams and serums, the absorption rate of the beneficial ingredients will be 100 to 1000 times more effective.

Dermastamp – E-Dermastamp

E-Dermastamp is a vibrating stamping device which has adjustable needles which penetrate the skin. It is a development evolved from the Derma Roller but is more comfortable and less painful. In most treatments, the skin is first cleaned and then a numbing cream applied, then the Derma Stamp glides over the skin creating minute channels. It is designed to treat fine lines and wrinkles, reduce pore size, improve hyper-pigmentation and acne scarring while simultaneously activating collagen production. The treatment usually takes around an hour and a half and there is little downtime with only a slight reddening of the skin which usually lasts between 12 and 24 hours. The results are instant and improvements continue for a number of weeks.

Diamond & Platinum Skin Care Products

Diamond & platinum are being incorporated into serums, creams and general treatments to assist in the endeavour of eradicating wrinkles because their Nano particles have an extraordinarily efficient absorption rate. In beauty products they chemically attach themselves to the active anti-aging components within the product, allowing for deeper penetration, which equates to a much better result for the user.

Black diamond microspheres are used in order to transport the products' active ingredients – usually Vitamin C, hyaluronic acid, collagen and arbutin – to deeper layers of the skin, allowing them to reach cells that need rejuvenation.

Platinum works on a cellular level, to neutralize the build-up of toxins within the skin, leaving it looking radiant. Colloidal platinum restores the electrical impulses within the cells contained in the epidermis level, making them more resistant to free radical damage.

Diamond Peel Facials

These are treatments currently being offered by many spas. They use a machine containing crushed diamonds in order to resurface the skin. There are a number of home use treatments available that contain diamond powder to exfoliate and brighten the skin's surface.

DNA Anti-Aging Serum – Geneu, The Brand

The Revolutionary Anti-Aging Serum is now being tailored to your own DNA.

In the London suburb of Mayfair, there exists a boutique, which is fitted out to resemble a space-age capsule. It is called Geneu. It is a world first, bringing a revolutionary skin-care treatment that is based on over-the-counter genetic testing.

Geneu, the brand, was founded by a Professor Chris Toumazou and Nick Rhodes who met each other on a plane. Professor Chris Toumazou is regarded as a certified genius. He is best known for inventing the Cochlear Implant for the deaf, and the wireless heart monitor, along with an artificial pancreas. Nick Rhodes is better known as a member of the rock super group, Duran Duran.

On entering this boutique, you begin the process by filling out a comprehensive lifestyle questioner. Then you have a swab of saliva taken from your mouth. This sample is then dipped into a reagent, which breaks down the cells, allowing the DNA to be removed. Then the DNA is copied onto a microchip and analysed.

Two specific gene elements are screened for: the collagen breakdown, which equates to wrinkles, and the levels of existing antioxidant protection. The results are then analysed, and a serum is produced which targets both of these elemental breakdowns with the ingredients hyaluronic acid, peptides, vitamins, plus SPF, that fits your unique genetic profile, not just your skin type. This patented technology can, in thirty minutes, analyse the information and deliver a truly unique and personalised prescription for you.

Exercise Can Slow Aging

Research now shows that moderate, but regular, exercise expands part of the brain that shrinks with age. Scientists now believe regular, light physical activity is one of the best ways we can prevent the aging process. Walking briskly for 30 minutes a day, 4 times a week, is all it takes for us to regrow areas of our brains that are responsible for physical and psychological decline. So, therefore, we can substantially improve our brain's function by modest amounts of regular exercise.

Why is this so important? Because until recently we thought that the decline in our brain's function was inevitable. We now know it is not. The longer we continue our exercise routine, the greater will be the brain's increase in volume. This research has a profound effect on negating age related mental illnesses such as Alzheimer's and Dementia. Though scientists tell us they don't fully understand this process of the brain increasing its volume, they think it is due to the blood-flow increase in the neurons or other cells.

Exfoliate

To exfoliate is to apply a given product to the skin in order to remove dead skin cells, which enables new skin to regenerate. This cleans and stimulates the skin and allows for better absorption of active ingredients which wakes up the cells' communication, leading to the production of collagen. Look out for fatty acids, peptides, antioxidants and liposomes in the products used – key to much more beautiful skin. Top dermatologists advise to exfoliate regularly with lactic acid as this dissolves dead skin gently.

E-Dermastamp

E-Dermastamp is a vibrating stamping device which has adjustable needles which penetrate the skin and is a development evolved from the Derma Roller but is more comfortable and less painful. In most treatments, the skin is first cleaned and then a numbing cream applied, then the Derma Stamp glides over the skin creating minute channels. It is designed to treat fine lines and wrinkles, reduce pore size, improve hyper-pigmentation and acne scarring while simultaneously activating collagen production. The results are instant and improvements continue for a number of weeks.

Face Masks

Modern day face masks originate from very ancient skin treatment practises that clean the skin at a deep level, drawing out impurities. They have recently risen in popularity due to new technology and the number of new products currently being released into the beauty market. Generally, face masks provide an intensive cleansing treatment for skin and enhance the effectiveness of the products used in one's daily skin treatment.

Fat Reduction & Skin Tightening

Non Invasive treatments that can achieve dramatic effects include:

- Liposonix fat reduction and skin tightening. Liposonix is a device that is relatively new to the U.S. market, but has been used in Europe for a number of years to get rid of fat cells permanently within selected problem areas. It is especially good for areas around the waistline and abdomen.

- Thermage skin tightening. It is a non-invasive treatment that uses a machine to deliver radio frequency energy into the deeper layers of skin, creating a heating action that immediately tightens skin and underlying structures. Is effective on the eyes, face and body.

Fillers

Dermal fillers are used in a clinical situation as an effective way to restore lost volume to the face such as enhancing cheek bones and lips. Once these fillers have been injected it usually takes approx. 4 weeks for them to settle down and give the desired result.

Fillers & Botox

These are two non-invasive procedures that are applied by way of injection. They both serve a useful purpose in producing different effects cosmetically.

Botox (Botulinum) is a protein

Fillers (Hyaluronic) are complex carbohydrates.

Botox products relax the muscles, resulting in the softening of the appearance of wrinkles.

Fillers serve to fill the skin's underlying layer, which lifts the skin's surface, by filling in wrinkles, contour lines, lips, and sculpting the face.

More and more people are combining the two procedures – fillers & Botox – as when combined they can produce an excellent younger looking appearance.

Fractional CO2 Laser Skin Resurfacing

Claimed to be the anti-aging breakthrough of the decade by many doctors, this is a laser skin-resurfacing treatment that incorporates the effectiveness of a traditional carbon dioxide laser, previously considered the standard for wrinkle removal. This new laser resurfacing technique uses beams of light energy to create very small holes in the skin's surface, which then activate the body's natural production of collagen, putting it on a fast track. What is revolutionary about this system is that it does not create any damage to the top layer of the skin, so achieves maximum results with very little recovery time required – it delivers "extraordinary results" without the harsh effect of earlier generation machines and their applications, and the effects of just 1 or 2 treatments last between 8 and 10 years.

Gene Technology

The science of Gene Technology is generating considerable excitement in the world of skincare. Gene Technology is the ability to observe the behaviour of skin care ingredients on the skins' genes, inclusive of those that actually slow down the process of aging. Beauty company technicians are now observing precisely how ingredients within skincare formulas effect the behaviour of our skins' genes, including in this process, the exact observation of the genes that assist in the slowing down of the aging process. In some cases to date, the results have been quite spectacular. So much so, that the effectiveness of some of the resulting products has been under-reported – because under present day legislation anything which modifies the way skin functions must be classified as a medicine, and as such a prescription would be required for these skincare products. We are now able to buy creams and serums that are tailor-made to our own skin cell structure.

Green Tea Extract

Tea is loaded with nutrients called Polyphenols. These have been shown to fight free radicals. It is also claimed that they can reduce sun damage, and protect our skin from developing cancer cells. It is recommended that you use green tea extracts under sunscreens in order to give your skin double protection. Polyphenols are available in creams and lotions, which may also slow signs of aging like reducing wrinkles and sagging skin.

Hair

We have about 100 thousand hairs on our head. Stress, diet, hormones and age all contribute to our hair becoming thinner.

Hair – Baldness Cure

There is now the prospect, that in the not too distant future, there will be an available treatment to cure baldness – that will actually work. For the first time, scientists have proven that it is possible to create entirely new follicles from which hair grows. "A ground breaking experiment suggests that it will soon be possible to reprogram the skin to sprout hair from scratch, allowing men and women who have lost, or are losing, their hair to regrow new hair." As it has long been believed that hair follicles are formed only in embryos, and therefore cannot be re-activated once lost, this new discovery has astonished scientists as it proves that new follicles, and as such new hair, can be grown from the cells within the skin.

A drug that can address these problems, by way of growing new hair, will probably be available within the next 5 years. This treatment could be used to address the problem of unwanted hair as well.

Hair – Kerastase

Is a density activator formulated with stem oxydine and vitamins B3, B5, and B6, and acts at a root level to target stem cells to awaken hair follicles in order to support hair growth. Results claimed are thicker, healthier hair, and up to 1700 new strands in 3 months. The serum also contains textured polymers for instant lift.

Hair – Minoxidil

Is the active ingredient, and top over -the- counter treatment, used today to promote new hair growth.

Hair New Machine Treatments

Machines that are using a combination of infra-red and antimicrobial technologies with ultrasonic vibrations, which work in achieving greater penetration of conditioners and vitamins into the hair shaft, have recently been introduced to some hair salons in Europe and the USA. The treatment breaks down a conditioner into Nano particles that allow for a much greater absorption rate within the cortex of the hair shaft. It is claimed that these systems work very well on badly damaged hair and hair that is frizzy due to perming and over bleaching. The entire head of hair can be treated and conditioned in 10 minutes.

Happy Horny Skinny Pill

It has been reported that Wellbutrin, described as The Happy Horny Skinny Pill, is an excellent drug for sexual dysfunction in both women and men and can be useful for women when taken like Viagra shortly before sex. It is claimed that Wellbutrin, or Bupropion, which primarily is marketed as an antidepressant, will assist weight loss and give your libido a lift. This drug works on norepinephrine, so it could well reduce appetite, and it increases dopamine and norepinephrine levels that relate directly to female sexual arousal.

Women who were suffering hot flashes, mood swings, depression, vaginal dryness and loss of libido, reported that after taking Wellbutrin for a month everything changed; no more dryness, increased interest in sex, a more balanced and elevated mood and being generally happier. They feel that their metabolism is functioning more efficiently, consequently losing weight without changing their diets or exercising more.

Herbs – Adaptogens:
The New Anti-Aging Stress Relievers

Are you a bit tired, stressed, and even run down? Then welcome to the club – as with our frantic lifestyle in this ever-increasingly connected world, is it any wonder? A new term for all of this is emerging, referred to as *Adrenaline Exhaustion* and this could be the very cause of our demise. The medical profession raise their eyebrows when this is suggested as they believe there is no evidence that your adrenaline glands crap out because of stress. They attribute the symptoms to other underlying conditions such as depression or sleep deprivation – or in other words, brain exhaustion.

So what is this *Adrenaline Exhaustion* all about? The Adrenaline glands sit atop our kidneys and produce a number of very important hormones which include oestrogen, cortisol, adrenaline and aldosterone which assist our bodies with dealing with stress as they regulate our metabolism and control our blood pressure.

Even though the medical profession acknowledge the importance of the adrenals to our health, the concept that these glands could become overworked and, as such, exhausted due to daily stress has created an ongoing debate for them.

Chinese and Indian medicine have used herbs as a treatment for this condition for some considerable time, believing that certain adaptogenic herbs, such as ginseng, rhodiola, ashwaegandha, liquorice, holy basil and schizanda berry combined with a healthy diet lifestyle and exercise regime can change this condition dramatically. There are a number of well-known celebrities that fully support this approach.

As many doctors just aren't aware of these different approaches, some patients who have suffered these symptoms described as *Adrenaline Exhaustion* and have received no improvement from conventional medicine have turned to the world of adaptogens. They are claiming remarkable results, reporting life changing effects.

Hormones

Hormones are one of the most important bodily functions we humans have. They stimulate, or inhibit, our growth. They control our sleeping cycles, and our mood swings, regulate our hunger cravings, and they activate, or restrict, our immune system. Further, they initiate our body's metabolism and mobilize our body's flight, fight, and mating activities. Moreover, they programme our cells, and are responsible for such cycles in our lives as: puberty, parenting and menopause. They control our reproduction, and that of our sexual arousal.

Growth hormones are a peptide hormone, which stimulates growth and encourages development in the human body. This peptide hormone is made up of 191 amino acids, and their cells are found in the pituitary gland within the brain.

Many of the functions of human growth hormones are still unknown, but what is known is that they can decrease body fat, increase muscle mass and bone density, and raise energy levels. We know that fasting, low blood sugar, vigorous exercise, and sexual activity can all stimulate the release of growth hormones.

The significance of hormones can never be under estimated in relation to aging and anti-aging – as they indeed make us who we are.

Hormones – Growth Hormones (HGH)

It has been touted as the "anti-aging breakthrough," – and further, it is claimed to: reduce body fat, increase lean muscle mass, boost our moods, give us plenty of energy, get rid of wrinkles, and tighten saggy skin, making us feel and look decades younger.

So what is HGH? It is a single-chain peptide hormone that is manufactured deep within the brain – for the most part within the pituitary gland. When it is released it travels via the bloodstream throughout our entire bodies. During this process it flows to our fat cells where it acts in shrinking these cells. It also travels into the cells within our muscles. The muscles then strengthen, giving them the appearance of being toned and tight.

As this hormone travels to our skin it helps in maintaining a healthy blood flow, and assists in the production of collagen, which in turn strengthens the underlying structures within the skin. It is claimed further that this process supports the skin's elasticity, keeping it firm, tight, and wrinkle free. These are the reasons that HGH is being hailed as the "youth hormone" and the key to combat aging.

While our bodies obviously manufacture HGH themselves, as we age these levels begin to decline rapidly, and until recently the way to increase HGH levels was with prescription injections that are very expensive – as much as $1500 a month. There is also considerable concern and criticism of these synthetic HGH injections as they could upset the body's natural production of HGH. *See also: Growth Hormone Therapy*

Hormones – Growth Hormone Therapy

Fast becoming the most popular anti-aging treatment in America today," Growth Hormone Therapy is often referred to as "The Youth Hormone."

Science says that a 20 year old produces twice as much growth hormone in her body as she will when she turns 40.

So in theory, by increasing levels of HGH you will be turning back your body clock and, therefore, the aging process.

Until recently, prescription injections delivering synthetic HGH was the most common method. But this is at the expensive cost of some $1500 a month. After some twenty years of research into the best methods to promote pituitary health, the source of the body's growth hormones, oral compounds have been very recently created that are capable of increasing growth hormone levels of some 500%. The method used to achieve this is by way of a special blend of amino acids – HGH levels increasing by some five times.

Relatively, Dr Oz recently asked his TV audience, "How many of you want to start feeling 20 years younger right now?" He is quoted as saying, "I have been looking for ways of increasing HGH naturally because I don't like getting the injections." These statements created a frenzy, leading to a full blown phenomena, as the cost of this product that, " – may reduce wrinkles, tighten saggy skin, decrease body fat, increase lean muscle mass, strengthen bones and boost mood, while giving you plenty of energy and improve sex drive," is taken orally, for a cost of some $US100 a month. However, some medical professionals are saying that the benefits are based on research that's preliminary, though it appears that most parties do agree that HGH plays a pivotal role in our health and in our aging process.

Hormone Cream – Menopause

In 2012, a group of scientists presented research that showed that there was a natural oral compound capable of increasing growth hormone substantially. The formula that was developed subject to these research findings is now being sold internationally.

Research shows that the skin begins to deteriorate more rapidly during menopause due to a decrease in the levels of oestrogen. Of all the hormones our body produces, oestrogen has the greatest effect on our skin. It assists in the production of collagen, the protein that strengthens and gives elasticity to our skin. The research shows that 30% of collagen in our skin is lost 5 years after menopause, then continues to decline more slowly after that. A British Medical Journal report advised that by taking topical oestrogen therapy applied directly to our skin rather than taking a pill, an increase of collagen within the skin of some 48% was seen. Further International studies found that after 6mths use of a topical oestrogen, the skin became much firmer, and wrinkles decreased by some 70%.

Topical oestrogen therapy is simply a cream that contains oestrogen, which is applied to the skin – usually to the face. So now, essentially, we have available to us a hormone replacement therapy contained within a face moisturizer, which helps the production of collagen within our skin, giving it a new lease of life. New creams are now becoming available, which contain retinol, peptides and vitamins, as well as oestrogen.

HRT is usually dispensed by doctors in the form of pills or patches. By being available in a moisturizing cream, a whole new generation of skin care becomes available – as there is now convincing data that creams containing hormones help substantially in reducing wrinkles and the thickening of fragile skin.

Now we have available to us, a new generation of creams that do not contain synthetic or human hormones. Instead, they are manufactured using phytoestrogen extracts. A key phytoestrogen is genistein, which is derived from plants. The skin's receptors of oestrogen are fooled into believing that they are receiving genuine oestrogen, so block the enzymes which cause collagen depletion, when in fact they are receiving molecules of genistein, which is so similar to oestrogen that the receptors do not know the difference. Other forms of phytoestrogen are extracted from plants such as flaxseed, wheat germ, and soya, which can replicate the effects of normal oestrogen within our skin. For those that aren't happy about taking artificial hormones, now there's a credible alternative.

Hyaluronic Acid

Hyaluronic Acid draws out water from the dermis – the skin that lies below the surface. Look for a lotion that contains it as it has excellent hydrating qualities and promotes collagen production.

Hyper-Pigmentation

Hyper-Pigmentation is the appearance of excess, uneven melanin pigment in the skin. It occurs when the cells called melanocytes are damaged by sun, smoke, pollution, inflammation and hormones, resulting in the appearance of dark patches, freckles and blotchy spots. Hormonal change, oral contraceptives, pregnancy, or stress can also be contributing factors. There are a number of treatments that address these problems; topical fading agents, laser and light treatments, such as IPL (Intense Pulse Light), chemical peels, fruit acid peels, and Microdermabrasion.

Intense Pulsed Light (IPL)

IPL is a light based system used extensively for the treatment of sun damage, capillaries, pigmentation and general redness. The machine uses a beam of light with broad range of wave lengths which are directed to the dark or red areas of pigmentation in the skin. The light destroys the dark and red areas and over the following weeks a much more even complexion results.

Intracel Radio Frequency

This system is delivered via micro needles for specifically focused treatments. It heats up the skin which begins the process of rejuvenating the cells. It is very good for sagging skin and for stretch marks.

IV Vita-Infusion Facial

This treatment involves a cocktail of high potency vitamins & minerals being delivered intravenously. A registered nurse mixes this cocktail. The mixture usually consists of vitamins B12, B5, B6, B9 and vitamin C, as well as calcium & magnesium, and the uber antioxidant glutathione. As this is being absorbed into the body, a facial is administered to the client. The results are that some people feel energized immediately and others after a couple of hours – all feel really good and the skin looks great. After 2 or 3 treatments one sees a big difference in one's hair and nails. The cost is approximately $300-$340.

Las

The prescription drug Latisse that fattens skinny lashes, which get thinner as we age. Coconut oil applied to the lashes at night helps to treat breakages.

Lasers – Age Rejuvenating Technologies

In the serious quest for better age-rejuvenating procedures, nowhere can the search be better highlighted than in the advancements in Laser Technologies. We could be seeing a new dawn where plastic surgery is becoming obsolete because there is no need for the cutting & stitching, and Botox along with the funny faces is no longer on our radar screens as the face can be rejuvenated without any dramatically unnatural looking changes.

Lasers emit beams of light that are designed to target cells deep within the skin so as to stimulate collagen while leaving the surface skin unharmed. Fraxel and other types of fractional lasers use beams of light energy to create thousands of minute holes in the skin's collagen layer. This restores collagen and elastin to the skin cells while removing any excess pigmentation, broken blood vessels and laxity. These powerful beams of light can improve the appearance of wrinkles, sun damage, acne scars and laxity of the skin with very little risk of any scarring and downtime, the end result being a glowing and refreshed new you with tighter, smoother skin, and an evenly toned complexion.

Lasers – Eye Procedures

Lasers can be used in treatment of:

- droopy upper eyelids
- puffy lower eyelids
- double eyelids
- asymmetrical upper eyelids
- wrinkles and dark circles under the eyes
- crepe-like skin on lower eyelids

Lasers – Fractional CO2

Claimed to be the anti-aging breakthrough of the decade by many doctors, this is a laser skin-resurfacing treatment that incorporates the effectiveness of a traditional carbon dioxide laser, previously considered the standard for wrinkle removal. This new laser resurfacing technique uses beams of light energy to create very small holes in the skin's surface, which then activate the body's natural production of collagen, putting it on a fast track. What is revolutionary about this system is that it does not create any damage to the top layer of the skin, so achieves maximum results with very little recovery time required – it delivers "extraordinary results" without the harsh effect of earlier generation machines and their applications, and the effects of just 1 or 2 treatments last between 8 and 10 years.

Lasers – Fraxel Laser

The most used brand name in a clinical environment is the Fraxel Laser which uses specific wave lengths of light to stimulate the production of collagen or elastin. Its used in a variety of different treatments including wrinkles, sun damaged skin and scarring. After this treatment expect a week of downtime as the skin peels, flakes and is quite red after the procedure.

Lasers – Fraxel Skin Solutions

Fraxel is a laser treatment that can improve the appearance and youthfulness of skin. A range of lasers used to target specific issues include:

- Fraxel Restore, which treats uneven skin tone and clears most pigmentation. Lasers with various intensities that can remove most acne scars, surgical scars and capillaries, and refine pores, are also available.

- Fraxel Repair, which tightens skin on the face, neck, chest, breast and abdomen. It reduces wrinkles and can improve the appearance of stretch marks and scars.

Lasers – Home Use Machines

Personal lasers – small hand held devices – are now available for home use. Now you can visibly restore your skin's natural luminosity and smooth hard-to-treat wrinkles around the eyes at home.

These lasers have the same interaction with the skin that one obtains from a professional procedure by a Dermatologist, though getting results takes more time than from the more potent, in-house clinical lasers. Disciplined use rebuilds collagen beneath the skin's surface for a more youthful and radiance appearance in as little as 2 weeks. Clinical studies and trials show that 95% of people who tried home lasers saw much smoother skin. Users have reported that their crows feet receded, blotchiness and sun damage disappeared, the face looks younger with tighter skin and even tighter eyelids.

Lasers – Inner Laser Lift

Dermatologic surgeon, M. Christine Lee – East Bay Laser + Skincare Centre, California, co-developed a new procedure, *The Inner Laser Lift,* which makes tightening nasolabial folds almost that easy.

Rather than using the laser on the surface of the face, Lee aims it at the inner cheek, tightening the underlying tissue from inside the mouth – a technique developed through dental research wherein an unexpected side effect of smoother, tighter skin was noticed.

Working with her husband, Luis Mansilla, a Neurologist and Laser Researcher, Dr Lee developed a hand piece for the laser that allows it to be used intra-orally, focusing its energy into soft tissue for maximum penetration.

The positive results of the Inner Laser Lift usually last about a year – annual follow up enough to maintain these results indefinitely. And it is painless – all you feel is a puff of heat.

Lasers – Neck Lift

A laser neck lift includes the removal of fat from the jowls and under the chin using liposuction. It addresses sagginess by lifting the skin and muscles, which improves the contours of the face and the prominence of the cheeks without leaving any obviously visible scars.

Lasers – Photo Rejuvenation Facial

The Laser Picosure is used in the "Photo Rejuvenation Facial," that doctors are now performing, using this laser with less ouch-inducing. The Focus Lens Array is an add on to the Picosure that redistributes the Picosecond beam into hundreds of micro beams to smooth the skin and even out tone. After 4 treatments patients had a 50-75% reduction in wrinkles and hyperpigmentation. On a scale of 1 to 10, patients reported a pain level of 2, with 2 to 4hrs to recover.

Lasers – Skin Acne

The sebaceous glands that form acne are deep beneath the surface and hardly visible. In order to get into the sebaceous gland, gold is used with the laser device. This innovative procedure involves massaging fine gold coated sand into the skin, which is then treated with a hair removal laser. The gold absorbs the laser's light, converting it to heat, which renders oil glands inactive. Clinical studies show, on average, a 61% drop in inflammatory lesions.

Lasers – Tattoo Removal

Cleaner tattoo removal in half the time by using the Picosure Laser that pulses light much more quickly than typical lasers, breaking down ink into smaller pieces, which are easier for the body to absorb.

Lasers – Vaginal Rejuvenation

The SP Dynamic hand piece that is used intra-orally, by Dr Lee, focusing its energy into soft tissue for maximum penetration, used for the face, forehead and brow lifts, and to tighten the arms, stomach and thighs, is now being used for vaginal rejuvenation. This laser is going to make other vaginal rejuvenation treatments obsolete – because it's quick, painless, and has almost no side effects.

L.E.D. High Tech Miracle Mask

Even though L.E.D. Systems have been available for beauty treatments for some time now, their evolution and development is very much ongoing, the latest development being a Korean designed L.E.D. Mask. It is claimed, this L.E.D. Mask eradicates fine lines, improves skin tone, prevents aging – and is life changing.

A big part of its attraction is that it has both red and blue light spectrums in the one device, and is able to combine them at the one time. Because of its shape, the mask's contour fits over the face entirely, which allows a much greater coverage at one time than other systems. It has been described as a phenomenal tool.

L.E.D. Light Therapy

This is a treatment that uses L.E.D. Light Machines that produce a narrow wave length of blue or red light – the blue light function kills bacteria, and the red light function addresses anti-aging by stimulating the skin into producing elastin and collagen. L.E.D. Light Therapy works by way of light emitting diodes, which send measured wave lengths of light energy into the deeper layers of the skin, painlessly, either by way of red or blue light. The red light spectrum stimulates collagen and elastin production, which plumps wrinkles and smooths the skin, while the blue light source from these devices kills bacteria such as the source of acne. These devices are available for both clinic and home use applications, many coming in the form of handheld devices.

Line Freezing Creams

Revance Therapeutics, a Silicon Valley firm, has developed a pharmaceutical that uses the same components as Botox, which is applied as a gel instead of by injection with a syringe. Research of this product shows that when used on crows feet the gel elevated the ends of the brow by some 20%. The effects have been shown to last 2 to 3 months. It is not as strong as injectable Botox, but makes a significant difference. This product will be available soon, but as it is classified as a drug, a prescription will be required.

So, how do you get the same effects of Botox without using a botulin-toxin molecule which is classified as a drug and requires a prescription? There are some exciting developments in this field with the arrival of the so called "line freezing" creams. These creams work on the form of a dual encapsulated peptide that travels directly to where the nerve and muscle fibres meet. When they do, it mimics how botulinum toxin works, by breaking down Snap 25 – a complex in the skin that tells the muscle to contract. Used twice daily for a week, the results begin to show. It doesn't pack the potency of pharmaceuticals, but does assist significantly in making your skin tighter.

Liposonix

Liposonix is a device that is relatively new to the U.S. market, but has been used in Europe for a number of years to get rid of fat cells permanently within selected problem areas. It is especially good for areas around the waistline and abdomen.

L-ascorbic Acid

This is simply another word that means Vitamin C. Vitamin C boosts our immune system when taken internally. As a skincare product it becomes more complex due to its unstable and volatile nature. When exposed to air it undergoes a process of oxidisation and becomes ineffective. Vitamin C, when stable, is an important antioxidant that helps build collagen, reduces inflammation and promotes elasticity. How can we tell whether Vitamin C is stable? Look for L-ascorbic Acid in the list of ingredients.

Micro-Dermabrasion

This treatment uses tiny rough grains to buff and exfoliate the skin which unblocks pores and removes dead skin cells. Diamond crystals or salt are usually used in this process. It is used to treat wrinkles, fine lines and acne problems.

Micro-Dermaplaning

This system uses a specialized dermaplane blade - similar to a surgeon's scalpel. It exfoliates the skin's dead cells and removes the fine hair on the face. The treatment usually takes about 20 minutes and is painless with only a little redness (in some people) which tends to settle down in a few hours.

Natural Plant Power

Huge investments are being made in advanced research to prove that plants have true anti-aging powers. Several companies have launched high-tech skincare products, formulated on plant based face oils containing rosehip and chia seeds, which are extremely high in essential fatty acids. It is claimed, that as they are so similar to our own skin's lipids, they can heal and nourish our protective lipid barrier, and also play a part in the skin's rejuvenation – as a lack of unsaturated fatty acids ages cells and skin.

Nature & Longevity

Research now shows that: not only does walking treat the symptoms of depression, but where that physical exercise takes place makes a considerable difference. It has been shown that a walk in a natural environment, like a bush reserve or a beach, will lift your spirits – as opposed to a walk around the shops in a mall, which could make you further depressed. The research from the British Mental Health Organization, "Mind," claims that Echo Therapy – restoring one's health through connecting with a natural environment – has considerable benefits for our health and longevity.

Niacinanide & Niacin

Is Vitamin B3. It stimulates new collagen production in the skin, lightens sun spots and increases the skin's hydration.

Nightingale Droppings

Nightingale Droppings, the basis for Japanese Geisha facials, has been used for hundreds of years. It gives the skin a lovely shine and a very lucid glow.

Non-Surgical Facelift – The Silhouette Instalift

The Silhouette Instalift is said to be a straightforward procedure that painlessly lifts sagging skin, delivering very natural results.

The procedure is carried out in less than an hour and doesn't involve any cutting or stitches. It involves a doctor placing & pulling threads under the skin to lift the sagging from the neck, the chin, and the cheekbones. A fine needle is used to make a dot-size hole under the skin near your nose, from where threads with minute cones are threaded both up & down the face in a V shape. These threads self-attach to tissue, lifting it without the need for hooks etc. Over time, they cause the body to produce more collagen, and in about 6-8mths dissolve, leaving the face lifted for the next 1-2yrs. The results are considered excellent.

Non-Surgical Facelift – The Y Lift

A Dr Yan Trokel, Manhattan, does what he refers to as his Non-Surgical Facelift – The Y Lift. The Y Lift is about structural volumizing. Dr Trokel rebuilds the foundation of the face by injecting liquid fillers. In order to guide him, he takes pictures and drawings of the face. He then administers 4 shots of Novocain, makes 4 tiny needle holes, one next to each ear and 2 along the jawline, then inserts a surgical instrument which allows him to get deep enough to lift the muscle and put filler right on top of the bone. He injects Juvederm, a Hyaluronic Acid filler, which offers good longevity, is reversible, and metabolizes in the body naturally. He injects some 12 syringes, beginning from the cheeks and works down to the jawbone. He fills both cheeks, then moulds and contours the filler with his hands, then the jawline, then repeats the procedure. This procedure takes about half an hour and is painless. The before and after photos on Dr Trokel's website are a fair representation of the results to be expected – they are quite impressive.

Non-Surgical Facelift – Vitamin Injection Facials

This is a new treatment. It combines two well-known systems – Micro-Needling and Mesotherapy. Micro-Needling is a system that makes tiny punctures beneath the skin's surface, initiating a natural repair process, boosting collagen production. Mesotherapy injects a cocktail of vitamins & caffeine into cellulite.

This process involves hundreds of superficial needle pricks, which allows a cocktail of supposed "complexion perfecters" to seep into your skin. Many believers rave about the youth enhancing benefits of having syringes of vitamins and antioxidants injected into their faces.

This vitamin-needle treatment is marketed under different brand names, but all use similar serums, which are injected manually at differing depths and speeds of individual punctures. The injected serums, made up of the claimed skin perfecting formulas, are generally vitamins A1, B2, B4, B12, C, D, and E, as well as Hyaluronic Acid, and minerals: Zinc, Copper, Manganese, and Selenium – but these can vary between plastic surgeons and dermatologists.

Organ construction: 3D Printing Organ construction

This is the use of 3D printers to construct bodily organs. It's already possible to use 3D printers to construct organs, and it appears that it is now only a matter of time before we all have access to the technology of using 3D printers to construct bodily organs, in order to replace our sick or failing ones.

O-Shot: Revitalized Sex

The O-Shot (Dr Charles Runels) is an all-natural and painless non-surgical procedure using platelet-rich plasma, using one's own platelets and growth factors, isolated from a small amount of one's own blood, which is injected into the inner walls of the vagina. This treatment is claimed to rejuvenate and revitalize sexual function, giving one a dramatically improved sensitivity and sex drive.

Peptides

Peptides are small proteins which stimulate the production of collagen. This is at the forefront of anti-aging skin technology. The more recently released peptide formulas contain growth factor ingredients which increase the turnover of cells within the skin. By stimulating them, the skin begins to look much younger.

Plant Based Peels

This is an intensive treatment for people of any age who have differing skin concerns or who simply want to improve the skin's quality. It uses plant based products to exfoliate the skin and peel away the upper layers.

Priapus Shot: Better Sexual Performance

The Priapus Shot (Dr Charles Runels) is a treatment to help improve erectile dysfunction and sexual performance.

Radio Frequency (RF)

The rays penetrate the deeper dermal layers to stimulate collagen fibres, resulting in tighter, smoother skin. The treatment can go below the face, to uplift sagging neck skin, to tone the stomach, thighs and buttocks. Treatment options range from mild to medium to intense. Sublime-Refirne falls within the mild catergory: 3-5 sessions, spaced 3-4 weeks apart in order to gain results. In the medium catergory is Thermage CPT – this is regarded by clinics as the big gun. Results prove this RF Treatment improves the appearance of sagging skin in just one session. In the intense catergory, is the latest Ultra Therapy – this employs Ultra Sound technology to target the dermis and stimulate collagen production. Only one treatment is required and patients are impressed with the results.

Radio Frequency – Micro Needles

Radio frequencies are delivered through micro needles. The skin is heated up to start the cell regeneration process, and then problem areas like sagging and stretch marks are targeted in a very precise manner.

Resveratrol

Calorie restriction has been referred to as being the real fountain of youth. There is now an abundance of evidence that calorie restriction greatly reduces our chances of developing serious diseases, and scientists who are usually cynical about anti-aging claims, actually agree that this method does indeed work as it allows our body cells to cleanse and revitalize themselves, and greatly reduces the risk of many diseases such as diabetes, cancer and heart disease. Through the research done into calorie restriction, scientists are investigating and testing naturally occurring compounds that mimic the effects of calorie restriction – such as Resveratrol that is found in red wine, for example – as they think these compounds may restrict aging. It is considered that through this research we could expand our lifespans by up to 15 years within the next 40 years.

Retinoids

Retinoids are deriviatives of Vitamin A, and are believed to work by increasing collagen production within the skin's layers, and to decrease the breakdown of existing collagen. They are available via prescription in the form of Renova or Retin A. They are also available in many over-the-counter products in a weaker strength – the ingredient listed in these products is Retinol. Scientific research has shown that even a weaker strength product containing 0.4% Retinol, applied 3 time a week, results in significant reduction of wrinkles in 30 weeks – and not in just certain age groups, as some of the trial participants were in their 80's.

Revance – Botox Gel

Revance is a botulinum toxin gel dabbed on the skin by a doctor. It works in the same manner that Botox injectable versions do without the needles.

Salicylic Acid

Is incorporated in many over-the-counter and prescription products as it is less irritating than Alph-Hydroxy Acid. It is used to exfoliate the skin for the purpose of reducing the signs of aging. We are advised that if you are allergic to Salicylates, which are found in Aspirin, do not use Salicylic Acid, and to be aware of any allergic reactions to any of these products, and seek emergency medical help if anything problematic appears.

Salmon Roe Extract

This works by way of an enzyme in the roe, which is discharged while the baby salmon is hatching. It acts as a very gentle exfoliate, which doesn't irritate or dry the skin. As Omega-6 is known for preventing heart-plaque, it is also eaten.

Salt Therapy

Also known as HaloTherapy or Dry-Salt Therapy, Salt Therapy uses a machine named a Halogenerator, which grinds warm salt into very small breathable particles, and distributes this dried salt into the air within an enclosed cubicle, referred to as A Salt Chamber. The dried salt penetrates the lungs and absorbs the impurities, breaking up mucus, which enables the coughing out of these toxins. The theory is that if you have clean lungs you can absorb more oxygen, which equates to more energy, that assists every organ within the body to function more efficiently, improving one's general wellbeing. The salt is said to emit negative ions, which promote relaxation by balancing out our exposure to positive ions that aggravate our nervous systems throughout the day by the use of cell phones, computers etc.

Serums

Serums have been around for some 20 years but have a mystery associated with them. Recently they have been developed to such a degree that they are amongst the most exciting products in the skincare and age-rejuvenating arena, and are now regarded as the big story in the marketplace.

Described as potent but pricey, they are reported to be extremely effective. They have been developed by chemists who have created them by the use of cutting edge ingredients, which are blended into these new formulations.

There is no scientific definition for what constitutes a serum but in general they are lightweight, water based gels or emulsions that are used to retain ingredients such as antioxidants, vitamins, hydroxy acids etc. Usually they come in bottles with eye droppers, allowing application of the correct doses. They tend to be very light in their construction, and glide over the skin effortlessly, so that several layers of varying formulas can be applied simultaneously, in order to address varying skin problems, such as wrinkles, dark spots and lack lustre appearance – basically everything you are having a problem with. It is claimed that serums give the active ingredients within them direct access to areas of concern – such as wrinkles, brown spots and pimples – without the interference that moisturizers can create.

Serum Ingredients

The most effective ingredients in serums tend to be: retinol which stimulates cell growth, vitamin C which assists in the protection of the skin against UV damage, exfoliates like lactic glycolic and alpha hydroxy acids, also benzoyl peroxide and salicylic acid are used to penetrate into the pores of the skin, which rapidly work to stabilize any breakouts.

Serums are stronger and a lot more concentrated than creams or moisturizers. For instance, vitamin C serum delivers far more antioxidants to the skin's varying layers than will a cream or a lotion.

The great advantage of serums is in the ability to layer complementary ingredients at any one time, which can be a very effective approach in the area of anti-aging. For example, a serum containing collagen boosting peptides can be used effectively with an antioxidant cream. Retinol paired with niacin is another very potent combination.

- Retinol, peptides or rhamnose to boost collagen production
- Vitamin C or hydroquinone – to lighten dark areas
- Sunscreens and antioxidants – used in the morning

- Serums that are labelled safe around the eyes used for crow's feet and under eye bags, which usually contain peptides, caffeine and weaker concentrations of retinol

As serums usually lack occlusive ingredients like petroleum, sheaf butter or lanolin, which seals water into the skin, a lotion or cream applied over the top is usually recommended.

Snail Mucus

Because it contains a collagen type protein, like all mucus, it can help to improve wrinkles. In a recent study, reported in the journal *Skin Pharmacology and Physiology*, it is confirmed that mollusc secretions were found to stimulate fibroblasts, and further, they were found to have antioxidant qualities, establishing that snail mucus does indeed have "skin regenerative qualities."

SPF-15 Sunscreen

An affordable, scientifically proven, anti-aging cream you can use today is simply any broad-spectrum SPF-15 sunscreen. It is claimed that after 3 months use you will see significant rejuvenating effects.

Stem Cells

Are stem cells the secret miracle that can turn aging skin back into youthful, vibrant skin? Experts acknowledge that we are rapidly moving towards a world in which we will be able to regenerate every organ in our bodies, including our skin, by way of stem cell technology, which someday soon will unlock medical cures that we have never thought possible. For instance, some dermatologists are using the solution of stem cell rich sheep placenta applied to patients' skin in order to hasten the healing process after microdermabrasion and after general cosmetic procedures. Stem cells are the talk of the cosmetic industry. Not since Retin1 has a product created such hysteria.

Stem Cell Technology Applications

Presently the focus is on the stimulation of our own self-renewing stem cells in order to assist in regenerating our skin. What is really exciting in this field is the technology that now exists, which can reprogram any stem cells to act like skin stem cells. The products previously available are creams that contain peptides and plant stem cells. It is reported that the use of these products dramatically plumps the top layer of skin, reducing wrinkles and assisting in tightening saggy skin.

Stem Cell Technology – Miracle Creams

Stem cell cream presently doesn't actually contain stem cells. They are based on botanical stem cell sources, which are proteins and growth factors that the stem cells produce. Our skin cells are stimulated into regeneration by way of messages to them by proteins and amino acids. Many dermatologists and cosmetic companies believe that through these proteins and amino acids – which contain growth factors, peptides and other signalling chemicals – lies the secret to our skin's rejuvenation and its youthfulness. However, more choices are appearing for us in the exciting world of miracle creams made from stem cells. One brand obtains its cells from their patients' very own fat tissue. Another brand uses a supply of eggs from women obtained from IVF clinics. The company fools the eggs into believing that they are already fertilized. Then stores these substances of proteins and amino acids, which are then added to their skin care range. What these stem cells contain in an unfertilized state is the wider spectrum of molecules, which are capable of signalling to the skin cells the messages that they require in order for them to produce collagen and elastin, and further stimulate fibroblasts and keratinocyte growth factors, which is why they're claiming to be getting such excellent results. An independent study reported 73% firmness in skin, a 93% improvement in hydration, and much more alive skin after 3 months use.

Stem Cells – Some Botanical Extractions

Since 2008 plant stem cells have been appearing in leading brands derived from grown cultures of chemicals produced from the cells. For example: extracts taken from an apple have shown to be able to stimulate and protect our skin cells. The apple stem cell formula stimulated cell growth and was UV protective. Most brands are now seeking to exploit the natural growth factors associated with stem cells using high grade botanical extractions. Guerlain claims that the molecule contained within one of their creams will promote a longer lifespan of a cell, and increase the communication between the cells – a process that keeps them youthful. Extracted from the rare Gold Orchid, the claims are that they work on youthful cells by increasing their energy levels, and as such their ability to communicate. Dior have developed a range that penetrates deep within the cells beneath the dermis layer to reach the fibroblasts, which is the key to increasing density and elasticity within the skin.

Stem Cell Storage & Genome Backup

Exploring the latest research in new technologies, genome mapping and stem cell treatments, there appears an anti-aging treatment inside one's own body – stem cells. Many doctors agree that stem cells are a key part of chasing youth. For the long term, stem cell storage, which works as a sort of rainy day insurance. The cells are extracted, preferably when the patient is on the younger side – around 30 is said to be a good age – and can then be used to boost an immune system or help to rebuild damaged organs later. It's important to store cells before they become irreparably damaged. To collect and store stem cells at a clinic costs some $15,000 for the initial extraction, then storage costs around $50 per month.

Stem cells aren't the only high-end solution. You may now obtain a complete backup of your genome from a skin sample and have it stored it for future use. It is claimed that "This technology has the potential to reverse, or even cure diseases and repair damaged tissues of your body." The program costs $60,000 plus storage fees of $5,000 for 10 years, or $25,000 for a lifetime.

Sugar – Another Cause of Wrinkles

Sugar ages our skin through a process called glycation, which creates glycotoxins that produce wrinkles – even if we have religiously used sunscreen. When sugar molecules exist in our bodies they attack our cells by attaching themselves to the fats and proteins within our bodies, creating the process known as glycation. This causes our protein fibres to become brittle and irregular. The proteins most at risk of glycation are the same ones which give us a youthful appearance – collagen and elastin. The outcome: wrinkles, sagginess, a pale skin complexion.

Suqqu

Suqqu is a Japanese brand, famous for its deep massage techniques that, it is claimed, helps the muscles tighten and keeps them toned, especially around the neck.

Tech Neck

Refers to the damage caused to our necks due to our addictions to smartphones. On average, a person checks their phone 150 times a day. This action creates noticeable creasing that forms around the chin and neck. It is recommended that you hold your smartphone or tablet at eye level to prevent double chins from occurring. Daily massages also help – a few minutes a day makes a difference as it helps the skin's drainage systems. There are also cosmetic procedures which are used to tighten the muscles in the neck, as well as injecting Botox and using specific repair creams.

Teeth – The Revolution of Self-Repairing Teeth

It is claimed that in the not too distant future - within 3 years - going to the dentist to have a tooth drilled and filled may be a thing of the past.

Scientists are developing a technique to rebuild teeth by the use of tiny electrical pulses. Known as Electrically Accelerated and Enhanced Remineralisation (EAER), this treatment uses a tiny electrical current to push minerals into the decayed area of the tooth which repairs itself without any need for drilling or injections. This new treatment encourages the tooth to repair itself by speeding up the natural movement of calcium and phosphate minerals in a damaged tooth. Not only can this device fight tooth decay, but it can also be used to whiten teeth.

Another method to be developed recently could see the end of fillings and the pain of root canal surgery altogether. The United States Government's Research Dental Team are using a blast of intense light from a laser beam that activates a chemical in the mouth, which in turn re-activates the stem cells within the tooth. The stem cells then reform new dentine – the hard core of a tooth – rectifying the rot within a 12 week period. The procedure to initiate the process of healing within the tooth takes only 5 minutes under a laser.

Teeth – Ultrasonic Cleaning

The new Ultrasonic Toothbrush produces about 84 million oscillations per minute, eliminating the need for any type of pressure when brushing. The sonic waves destroy bacteria altogether, and it is regarded as extremely efficient at removing plaque with the minimum amount of brushing. Add the latest sonic powered flossing machine and you have a superb home teeth cleaning regime.

Telomerase: TA-65 Telomerase

Telomerase is an enzyme that appears to extend the tips of the chromosomes – the telomeres in some cell lines. It is claimed that as telomerase can avoid aging in cells, it can be used to combat the aging process as we know it. Therefore, telomerase-based therapies to fight aging are presently being developed, and at least one product, TA-65, a natural product-derived telomerase activator is already available, studies showing positive results.

The Acne App

There is now an app in the marketplace used for treating acne through the new tele-medical services like Yoderm or the Spruce App. You go online, enter in the skincare problem you have, enclose pictures of the problem, and within 24hrs a qualified dermatologist will have a treatment plan available for you – even a prescription if necessary. Yoderm costs $59 per consultation, while Spruce is $40.

Thermage Skin Tightening

Thermage skin tightening is a non-invasive treatment that uses a machine to deliver radio frequency energy into the deeper layers of skin, creating a heating action that immediately tightens skin and underlying structures. It is effective on the eyes, face and body.

Ultrasound (HPU) – An Ultrasonic Revolution

High Intensity Ultrasound is a non-invasive treatment that uses the power of ultrasound to lift both the skin and the deeper layers of S.M.A.S. – muscles which previously were reached only by surgical facelifts. It uses high speed oscillations (electrical currents) powered by ultrasound waves. During this procedure, pulses of warm HIFU energy are directed deep under the skin, causing the muscle layer to contract, while the heat stimulates fresh new collagen close to the surface, making the skin firmer, more elastic and brighter. Double chins and jowls become a lot tighter, cheeks appear fuller, eyes look more open, and the results continue to improve 3 months after treatment.

Ultrasound – Face Cleansing & Defoliating Brush

Cleansing brushes powered by ultrasound that oscillate at more than 300 impulses per second, which clean and exfoliate the skin without damaging it by way of stretching it. The faster the waves are delivered by the brush to the skin, the gentler the treatment is.

Ultrasound – Personal Machine Application At Home

There are a number of home-use ultrasound machines available in the marketplace today. The applications of these portable ultrasound home-use machines vary widely, ranging from face-lift & wrinkle removal, to slimming &

fat removal, through to treating black spots, acne, and even skin whitening. Some are also available for therapeutic use. Many of these machines have other applications built in as well, such as LED and Infrared function. They generally operate at frequencies ranging from 1-3 MHz.

Ultrasound – Ultrasonic Facial

The Ultrasonic Facial is a treatment usually offered in the Beauty/Spa environment. A moderately powerful ultrasonic system is used, rejuvenating the face by way of the removal of older and dead skin cells by exfoliation. High speed oscillation electrical currents, powered by ultrasound waves, are passed over the skin's surface, followed by a facial massage that drains away the impurities. Then, a serum containing antioxidants is applied to the face. The ultrasonic sound waves are again applied to the face to break down the serum into Nano particles, which allows a much deeper absorption and penetration of the serum to occur, markedly rejuvenating the skin.

Ultrasound – Ultratherapy System:
The Non-Surgical Facelift

The most powerful ultrasound system – the Ultratherapy System – is used by a doctor in clinic. It uses focused ultrasound waves to heat deep layers of skin tissue, which in turn stimulate collagen production, while bypassing the skin's surface. The system permits the doctor to view the areas that require treatment in detail via a screen, which then allows him to direct the ultrasonic waves precisely to those areas. This is referred to as *The Non-Surgical Facelift,* and has FDA approval for the tightening and lifting of the skin cells on the brow, the chin and neck. It is claimed to be the best non-invasive tightening device available, working principally on collagen production, which takes time to develop. As such it takes some 2 – 3 months for the extent of the positive effects to be seen on the skin cells but these effects do last for at least a year. It is claimed that after this treatment a large percentage of clients need no further treatment due to its success as the results are generally quite spectacular.

Vagina Revitalization – Rejuvenate Your Sex Life

A painless new treatment promises to revitalize the most intimate part of your body – and rejuvenate your sex life dramatically. Until now, kegel exercises, oestrogen creams for dryness, or tightening surgery which has a lengthy downtime and a risk of scarring, have been the only treatments available in this area, but during the past 18 months there have been about five new non-invasive treatments launched in the U.S. claiming to revitalize the vagina.

These pain-free systems use energies like radio frequency to stimulate collagen production and improve blood flow. A doctor inserts a probe that revolves 360 degrees around the vaginal canal, emitting pulses of energy. This results in the vaginal walls responding by releasing a rush of secretions, and a general increase of circulation within the blood cells and the nerves. Collagen creating cells are activated, which thicken and strengthen the vagina's walls.

The results reported have been extremely impressive. It is claimed that the benefits begin to be experienced within hours, and continue to improve for weeks. Patients report feeling wetter, tighter, more elastic, with more enjoyable friction during intercourse, with increased sensitivity generally, and heightened intensity of orgasms.

Vampire Facial

This is another trend – taking stem cells, or growth factors, from one part of the body and reintroducing them into the skin.

Kim Kardashian brought this technique, now known as "the Vampire Facial," into the limelight, wherein a serum that is made from one's own white blood cells is injected all over the face. There has been considerable criticism of this method by experts in the field, whose position is that you can't substitute one growth factor for another and expect it to work.

Vampire Series of Treatments – Improve Your Sex Life

Created by Dr Charles Runels, these are a trademarked series of treatments – The Vampire Breast Lift, The O-Shot, and The Priapus Shot – designed to rejuvenate the face, breasts, and genital area. All these treatments utilize platelet-rich plasma, using one's own platelets and growth factors, isolated from a small amount of one's own blood.

The Vampire Breast Lift uses a combination of fillers and platelet-rich plasma to enhance the cleavage between the breasts. This technique is used in the upper area of the breasts to plump and round them so these areas look their best when visible in bras and bikinis etc., and further helps in lifting the breasts generally. The procedure takes about 20-30 minutes.

The O-Shot is an all-natural and painless non-surgical procedure using the same platelet-rich plasma, which is injected into the inner walls of the vagina. This treatment is claimed to rejuvenate and revitalize sexual function, giving one a dramatically improved sensitivity and sex drive. The Priapus Shot is a treatment to help improve erectile dysfunction and sexual performance. Many couples choose to have both treatments – O-Shot and Priapus Shot – at the same time.

Vitamin C

Scientific research overwhelmingly supports vitamin C as being an excellent anti-aging product, which stimulates collagen and improves wrinkles, skin texture and its density. Vitamin C is one of the most important ingredients that can be used in cosmeceutical skincare today, and it is believed by some to be the fountain of youth. Direct application to the skin is excellent for brightening the skin, in addressing sun damage and healing the skin's surface generally. It can actually repair and prevent the visible signs of aging. The best range of skincare products and formulas tend to use Ascorbic Acid, being the most stable form of vitamin C. There are a further number of derivatives used – such as Ascorbyl Palmitate, Ascorbyl Phosphates and Ascorbyl Tetraisopalmitate – as most of these are a lot more stable than pure L-ascorbate vitamin C.

Vitamin Infusion Facials

This is suitable for all skin types and involves the infusion of a variety of vitamins into the skin. It assists in treating fine lines, pigmentation, sun damage, scar tissue, acne scarring and cellulite on the body. There are a variety of different systems in this category and different machines are used to greatly enhance the penetration of the vitamins into the skin.

Weight Loss – Endo Barrier

Made by G.I. Dynamics, this is another gastric device new to the market. It is a thin plastic sleeve that's inserted through the mouth into the top of the small intestine. The sleeve is secured in place and is left there for a year. Food passes through the sleeve but the calories do not get absorbed until they are further down the intestine. The device changes the release of hormones – like insulin – in the stomach, which helps reduce one's appetite and regulates blood sugar levels. It has now been used for some 6 years and results show that patients lose on average 20% of their body weight in 12 months.

Weight Loss – Green Coffee Bean Extract (GCB)

Also referred to as The Wonder Pill, Green Coffee Bean Extract is a natural component of the coffee bean – Chlorogenic Acid (GCB.) It is claimed that, "GCB interferes with fat storage and glucose absorption and that it specifically gets in the way of 2 enzymes that control fat cell storage, Lipoprotein and hormone-sensitive Lipase. In a recent research study, 16 people who took GCB changed nothing about their diets, yet all lost, on average, some 18 pounds – and 12 of the16 saw a heart-healthy reduction in their resting pulse, with no side effects reported.

Weight Loss – Liposonix

Liposonix is a device that is relatively new to the U.S. market, but has been used in Europe for a number of years to get rid of fat cells permanently within selected problem areas. It is especially good for areas around the waistline and abdomen. The Liposonix system uses high intensity focused ultrasound energy to non-invasively destroy targeted fat. It is claimed to produce predictable and uniformed results after a single 1 hour treatment.

Weight Loss – Maestro

Recently approved by the FDA, Maestro is claimed to be a weight-loss breakthrough. There is a nerve within our body that instructs our brain whether we are hungry or whether we are full. The Maestro is a device which interrupts these signals before they reach the brain. The device is like a small pace-maker, which is surgically implanted within the stomach. It sends electrical impulses to the vagus nerve – the nerve running from our brain to our stomach – which signals to the stomach whether it is empty or full. Research has proven positive results.

Weight Loss – Matcha

Matcha is a rich green tea extract in the form of fine powder. Research has shown that the compound, EGCG, an antioxidant catechien abundant in Matcha, boosts one's metabolism, and fat cells stop growing – likely due to its effect on leptin, the satiety hormone. While researchers have found it difficult to precisely determine how much EGCG is required in order to lose weight, it is generally now assumed that drinking 3 cups of Matcha a day should begin to produce positive weight loss in 3 weeks.

Weight Loss – Obalan: The $4000 Diet Pill

This is a gastric device in the form of a pill that makes you thin. The pill has a deflated balloon in it called the Obalan. It works by swallowing the pill that has a thin tube attached to it. When it is in the stomach, a doctor inflates the balloon with gas via the attached tube, which is then disconnected. The balloon works simply by making you feel full, and lasts for up to 3 months. After 3 months the balloon is deflated and removed through the mouth. Recorded results have been impressive with an average of 50% reduction in unwanted weight.

Weight Loss – Paris Freeze

Paris Freeze is the latest scientifically proven technology that destroys fat cells by way of freezing them. The procedure is used on the stomach, thighs, hips and arms.

After the fat cells are frozen they are then naturally broken down by the body within a matter of weeks. This procedure is a non-invasive treatment that takes about 25 minutes to complete. There is no pain and no downtime and, as such, certainly falls under the category of a lunchtime procedure.

Weight Loss – Ultra Lipolyse Treatment

Ultra Lipolyse Treatment uses lasers to break down fat cells and then tighten the skin. A skilled practitioner, usually a doctor, competent in the use of these lasers, can reshape body areas, smoothing away lumps and bumps on the legs, back and hips. This procedure is excellent for stomachs and bottoms, and can also be used for calves, knees, upper arms and jawlines. The new generation of these lasers achieve excellent results with very little pain.

Weight Loss – Vanquish

Vanquish is the latest fat removal technology. It is claimed to be a major technology breakthrough. It falls under the non-invasive category, and can treat large surface areas of the body uniformly, is efficient, comfortable, fast, with no pain, and patients feel only a warm sensation that they report as "very relaxing."

The machine is placed about an inch above the area to be treated. Radio frequency waves are transmitted that can differentiate between fat, skin and muscle cells. The heat causes cell-death within the fat cells, rendering some to be killed instantly, with others dying off within a matter of weeks. The dead fat cells are then passed through the body, filtered out through the lymphatic system, metabolized within the liver, then eliminated through the urine. Because the fat cells are killed off, the fat loss will prove to be permanent.

Researchers found that Vanquish can kill up to 60% of the fat cells treated, and the results are visible within 2 weeks. It is claimed to be, "The safest, easiest way yet to remove fat." There is no pain, no downtime, and is regarded as inexpensive, being in the $400 - $800 price range for the 30 minute treatment. It usually takes 4 sessions to obtain the desired results. It is currently designed for use in the stomach area and for love handles. No doubt it will be adapted to treat other areas of the body very soon.

Wellbutrin

It has been reported that Wellbutrin, described as The Happy Horny Skinny Pill, is an excellent drug for sexual dysfunction in both women and men and can be useful for women when taken like Viagra shortly before sex.

It is claimed that Wellbutrin, or Bupropion, which primarily is marketed as an antidepressant, will assist weight loss and give your libido a lift. This drug works on norepinephrine, so it could well reduce appetite. It increases dopamine and norepinephrine levels, which relate directly to female sexual arousal.

Women who had menopausal symptoms, or had a hysterectomy, and were suffering hot flashes, mood swings, depression, vaginal dryness and loss of libido, reported that after taking Wellbutrin for a month everything changed. They reported no more dryness, increases in their interest in sex, a more balanced and elevated mood and being generally happier. They feel that their metabolism is functioning more efficiently, consequently losing weight without changing their diets or exercising more.

Wrinkle Free Fillers – New Injectables

A youthful look can be enhanced through the use of a permanent filler for deep lines, and anti-wrinkle injections for more shallow lines. Recently the FDA approved 4 fillers: Perlane, Juvederm, Artifill and Radiesse - Restylane was approved in 2003 – each of these products use slightly different substances to fill wrinkles. What's significant is we can now use these fillers to volumize skin anywhere on the face, so you can really sculpt a lifted, youthful look without surgery. A facelift pulls the skin tight, whereas fillers add volume to the face, giving it a more youthful and natural look.

Research now shows that injected fillers that contain hyaluronic acid such as restylane and juvederm created vigorous new collagen production. Emervel is a highly hyaluronic acid filler. The molecules in this formula are very fine in substance, and are injected closer to the skin's surface, without puffiness. It gives longer lasting very natural results. Most of these fillers last for approximately 12 months or longer.

Xeomin

Is a botulinum toxin type A. It is a pure form of the toxin. It is produced without protein additives so there is less risk of adverse reactions and tolerance build-up. It is used in combination with Botox and Dysport to soften lines on forehead and to lift sagging skin around jawline.

Yoga Facial

This facial is an intense workout for the face. For 30mins your skin is stretched, lifted and pulled in a series of regulated, repetitive movements, which are performed very firmly. The concept behind this is that if you stimulate the skin, this will stimulate collagen and elastin production, therefore, strengthening and toning the facial muscles. Due to the many repetitive movements on the skin, the muscles beneath are being trained to stay strong, thus defying gravity.

Ancient Wisdoms Of The Mystical Traditions

Over the centuries extremely wild claims have been made in relation to extreme longevity. Throughout ancient texts there have been claims of people living for hundreds, and even thousands, of years. Ancient Indian texts record people living for hundreds of years, and The Bible records accounts of extreme longevity – ranging from Methuselah living to 969 years of age, Job to 210yrs and Joshua to 110. Chinese legend claims that Peng Zu lived for 800 years, and the Torah makes similar longevity claims, as do texts in Arabic cultures. According to ancient and modern alchemists, we humans are capable of complete control over our own bodies, including the process of immortality. There are claims that 14th century alchemists produced the elixir of life in the form of a drink, which ensured their immortality.

Presently, in developing countries the most prominent cause of death is the aging process itself. In the 2010 issue of Scientific American Magazine, the question is posed, "Why can't we live forever?" For hundreds of years some scientists have believed human aging was fixed, a process that had been programmed within our biology, which resulted in an inbuilt time of death. However, scientists now believe that this is in fact a myth and it is indeed possible to revise our own personal life span.

Occasionally, in the course of our research, we discover information which is of such significance, we believe that it warrants extended coverage for the record – and that it should be made available to our readers so that you may be fully aware of such important subject matter. The Action E-Book, *The Secret 60 Second Age Rejuvenation Process – The All Natural Way To Becoming Younger & Staying Forever Young,* stems from such research. A personal commitment to practicing the given method, called *The Secret 60 Second Age Rejuvenation Process* * that can be used in conjunction with – and is complemented by – any of *The Latest Age-Rejuvenation Products & Procedures,* enables us to more rapidly achieve the results we desire. To these ends, we sincerely hope that you flourish on your journey of age rejuvenation, irrespective of your present biological age.

So let's continue the journey to discover a new youthfulness – a new story for humanity – one that incorporates modern science with the ancient wisdoms of the mystical traditions.

*The Secret 60 Second Age Rejuvenation Process – The All Natural Way To Becoming Younger & Staying Forever Young, CreateSpace eStore: https://www.createspace.com/5664865

For the Website: Best of Age Rejuvenation, visit:
https://sites.google.com/site/bestofagerejuvenation/

For more Action E-Books, visit:
https://sites.google.com/site/actionebookpublications/

E-mail: actionebooks@gmail.com

n.b. Please always remember to continue your search for the products and treatments you identify with as being best suited to your needs by way of conducting your own searches on those areas of your particular interest, so you can gain information from those people who have already experienced the product or treatment and who write their views as to their results, for even though we take the greatest of care to accurately present the facts and information, these are simply a guide.

www.ingramcontent.com/pod-product-compliance
Lightning Source LLC
Chambersburg PA
CBHW062049280526
45788CB00003B/1168